I0470984

Excel Course

By Robert Stetson

TABLE OF CONTENTS

CHAPTER 1 WHAT IS EXCEL?

The intended purpose of a spreadsheet is to automate the process of doing matrix calculations in an accounting environment. Let's get that out of the way right now. It's not that complicated.

Let me show you how easy it is to put this magic application to work for you. I will walk you through the basics step by step and when it's over you will wonder what the fuss was all about.

Spreadsheets have been thought of as being the purview of accountants, with their pencils, sleeve-elastics and visors.

Courses in accounting can leave the student glassy-eyed with all the debits and credits and how either of these two words be a negative or a positive depending on the column and its relationship to other factors.

Spreadsheets are the simple common sense way to keep track of anything numeric in nature. The fact is; data is data.

I even use spreadsheets for non-numeric things because it is a convenient way to create tables containing information in an organized fashion. I'll talk more about non-numeric spreadsheets in Chapters 3, 4, and 9.

Once you begin to use spreadsheets, you will start to use them for just about everything.

CHAPTER 2 THE SPREADSHEET

THE UNDO COMMAND

Easily the most important command you will learn. Whenever you do anything and then stop cold with a blank face and say, "Oh no!" just press <Ctrl> and <Z> together and the last operation will be undone, "Whew!" This usually happens after 45 minutes of intense entries that will be lost because you goofed. I almost gave this paragraph its own chapter.

THE SPREADSHEET

Let's take a look at the standard spreadsheet layout. All spreadsheets are laid out this way.

Across the top you have the "X" coordinate, and down the left side you have the "Y" coordinate. It's the old Cartesian coordinate system you learned in high school Algebra.

Down the right side, you have the results for the items listed down the left, and across the bottom you have the results for items listed across the top.

Let me show you how that works below.

	MON	TUES	TOTAL SALES
FISH	3	4	7
BEEF	3	5	8
DAY TOTAL	6	9	15

Across the top we have the days of the week.

Down the left we have the product description.

Each box in the matrix shows how many of each different product was sold on each different day.

Across the bottom we have the total of all products for any given day.

Down the right we have the total for each product for all given days.

In the lower right hand corner is the total of all given products sold on all given days,

	MON	TUES	TOTAL SALES
FISH	6	4	10
BEEF	3	5	8
DAY TOTAL	6	9	18

If we increase our sales on Monday by three fish, what will happen to the total number of products sold on Monday and how will that affect the total sales overall? That is shown on the chart above.

	FISH	BEEF	DAY TOTAL
MON	3	3	6
TUES	4	5	9
TOTAL SALES	7	8	15

Let's reverse the headings across the top and down the left side.

You can see that it doesn't matter which way we arrange the days and the product identification. The results are the same. All we have done is reverse the orientation of the data. The totals remain the same.

	FISH	BEEF	DAY TOTAL
MON	6	3	9
TUES	4	5	9
TOTAL SALES	10	8	18

That's true when we make a change in the number of fish sold on Monday. The totals are the same as the first two charts shown above. The difference remains in the orientation of the data.

Please, bear with me through the simple things. I want to make sure everyone gets this concept.

So, how do we decide which items go across the top and which items go down the left side? That's the topic for the next chapter. The answer is simple.

CHAPTER 3 SPREADSHEET STRATEGY

There are basic rules governing the placement of headings for spreadsheets.

Let's imagine you need to track daily and weekly trends over the course of a month.

The trend measurements are of a finite number, let's say you measure four times a day. We know a month is between twenty eight and thirty one days. Knowing that, let's plot a matrix that is four columns by thirty one rows (4X31).

A matrix thirty one days wide would be very cumbersome. You can't fit it on an 8X11.5 inch sheet even if you print in landscape.

Imagine if you decide to extend the measurement to a year so you could extend the plotting of the trends.

Obviously, the days of the month headings go down the left and the headings for the readings go across the top.

Now you can group days into weeks and get sub-total averages per week and total averages for the month.

Even if you expand the number of samples per day to five or six, you can still manage to redesign the matrix to fit.

With the plan shown below you can extend the number of days out to three hundred and sixty-five and although you will have a yield of twelve pages, the data will still be manageable when you break the matrix down into one month per sheet.

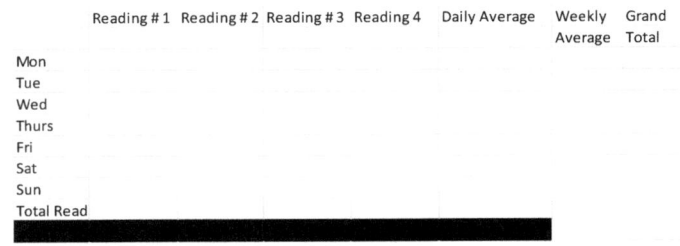

	Reading #1	Reading #2	Reading #3	Reading 4	Daily Average	Weekly Average	Grand Total
Mon							
Tue							
Wed							
Thurs							
Fri							
Sat							
Sun							
Total Read							

Each sheet would have its own monthly average and the twelfth sheet could be terminated using the annual average derived from the sum average of all twelve sheets.

When making a spreadsheet you can inject such things as barriers to make it easier to pick off the totals more easily. Here I have placed black rows to separate average readings to improve readability.

In the "Font" area of the "Home Tab" at the top of the screen, there is a college hat Icon. If you click on that the color pallet will drop down allowing you to select the desired color. I chose black.

Next put the mouse pointer on the square to the rightmost point where you want the background color to begin and drag the pointer to the left edge of the spreadsheet along that row. It will make all the blocks along that row the background color you have selected.

CHAPTER 4 FORMATTING THE SHEET

Next we're going to insert our first formula for automatically tracking averages. This is where most people get nervous. Let me show you how easy this is.

Click on the block intersected by the column marked "Daily Average" and in the row called "Mon". The block borders will become darker than the others. That means that this is the block you're working on.

Now, up top in the window with the symbol fx, called "f" of "x" or function of x, (you learned this in High School Algebra), type in an equal sign followed by the word "Average", followed by a left parenthetical symbol (no spaces).

Data in the row "Mon" extends to the right across four columns labeled "B" through "E". You can see the column names at the top just above the column headings you entered.

The row "Mon" is in the 3rd row down making it row 3. (The row numbers go down along the left of the spreadsheet next to the days of the week you entered.

The column letters and the row numbers identify each block of data. We want to average the blocks B3, C3, D3, and E3.

To average a series of block locations, you need only enter the starting block (B3) a colon and then the ending block (E3).

When you enter the values "B3:E3" notice that a long horizontal square appears spanning the blocks you identified in your formula.

Below, enter the right parenthetical to close off the equation and you're done.

The part you have just done is shown below.

The block where we entered the formula =AVERAGE(B3:E3) now has a small green triangle in the upper left and the block says "#DIV/0". That's good. It simply means that there is an error because the blocks have zero value and you can't divide by zero.

	Reading # 1	Reading # 2	Reading # 3	Reading 4	Daily Average	Weekly Average	Grand Total
Mon					#DIV/0!		
Tue							
Wed							
Thurs							
Fri							
Sat							
Sun							
Total Read							

Let's enter some numbers in those blocks and see what happens.

	Reading # 1	Reading # 2	Reading # 3	Reading 4	Daily Average	Weekly Average	Grand Total
Mon	50	22	50	22	36		
Tue							
Wed							
Thurs							
Fri							
Sat							
Sun							
Total Read							

By entering the values 50+22+50+22 and then finding the average by taking the total 144 and dividing it by the number of entries (4) we get an average value of 36.

You can change any of the numbers and the new average value will be automatically calculated and displayed.

I know what you're doing. You're looking at the big spreadsheet and mumbling, "Holey Moley!" that's a lot of typing, and you'd be right, but we're NOT going to have to do that.

	Reading # 1	Reading # 2	Reading # 3	Reading 4	Daily Average	Weekly Average	Grand Total
Mon	50	22	50	22	36		
Tue							
Wed							
Thurs							
Fri							
Sat							
Sun							
Total Read							

Put your mouse pointer on the square labeled "Mon" and press down on the left mouse button.

Hold the mouse button down and drag the pointer all the way down to the empty square located after the black row and under the words "Grand Total".

Release the mouse button with the pointer in that square. The whole block of data should be dark except for the square labeled "Mon".

Now put the mouse pointer on the furthest square to the left where the word "Mon" should go just under the black banner at the bottom of the matrix.

Right click on the mouse and a drop down menu will appear next to the mouse pointer. Select the option with the little picture of a mountain and a sun.

When you click on that picture the area you highlighted will be duplicated as shown in the spreadsheet below.

Repeat this three more times and you have five weeks of spreadsheet.

The amazing thing is that all the coordinates you entered in the formulas for the first section are repeated, but with new numbers to correspond to the new position of the copied sections.

	Reading # 1	Reading # 2	Reading # 3	Reading 4	Daily Average	Weekly Average
Mon	50	22	50	22	36	
Tue					#DIV/0!	
Wed					#DIV/0!	
Thurs					#DIV/0!	
Fri					#DIV/0!	
Sat					#DIV/0!	
Sun					#DIV/0!	
Total Read	50	22	50	22		
						36
Mon	50	22	50	22	36	
Tue					#DIV/0!	
Wed					#DIV/0!	
Thurs					#DIV/0!	
Fri					#DIV/0!	
Sat					#DIV/0!	
Sun					#DIV/0!	
Total Read	50	22	50	22		
						36

You will need to clear out the old data in the replicated areas where you copied to, so you can enter the correct data.

The data block next to "Mon" with the entry "50" is where we will put our pointer and drag it down and to the right until it gets to "Sun" and over to column 4.

Right click on the mouse key and select "Clear Contents".

Be careful not to clear the contents in the blocks containing the formulas or you will have to retype them.

When you're done with the pasting and clearing of the one week blocks you will need to trim them down to anywhere from 28 to 31 days depending on the number of days in the month. For our example here I have trimmed the calendar to 31.

Now there's just one more thing to do. You need to create the means to display an average for the entire month. To do this, just click on the data block under the column called "Grand Total" and one row below the black bar at the end of the spreadsheet.

The formula for this square is "=AVERAGE(G11, G20, G29, G38, G43).

Above is the completed spreadsheet for a one month data study.

Up to now I have had you enter formulas limited to the "AVERAGE" function without much in the way of explanation.

CHAPTER 5 EXCEL FORMULAS

AVERAGE

The actual formulas are simple enough if you're using the spreadsheet for every day math, such as business math. If you're a Physicist, you need help.

You have been using the "=AVERAGE" operand up to now, but I'll restate the use of the average function.

To find the average of two or more locations that are not adjacent to one another, use the formula;

=AVERAGE(Xx, Xx, …) where "X" is the letter at the head of the column and "x" is the row number.

To find the average of two or more adjacent values, use the formula =AVERAGE(Xx:Xx) where "X" is the column and "x" is the row.

The locations can span any number of data locations and everything in between will be included in the average value.

The operand for a range of locations is the colon ":". The range can be used in the vertical or the horizontal direction.

	FISH	BEEF	DAY TOTAL
MON	6	3	9
TUES	4	5	9
TOTAL SALES	10	8	18
Average of 6, 3, 4, 5			4.5

What many people don't realize is that the averaging formula can be used for areas of numbers.

In the spreadsheet example above, we have taken the average spanning the blocks from "MON" and "FISH" to the location "TUES" and "BEEF".

You can see that the total sales were 18 units, but the average of your unit sales is the sum of "6+3+4+5" divided by the number of units (4) or "18/4" which equals "4.5".

So we have used the averaging operand across the diagonal span of values and captured more than one row and column in the equation. This can save you a lot of separate formulas where one would do.

ADDITION ($\sum$)
To find the SUM ($\sum$) of two or more locations that are not adjacent to one another, use the formula;

=SUM(Xx+Xx+…) where "X" is the letter at the head of the column and "x" is the row number.

To find the SUM of two or more adjacent values, use the formula =SUM(Xx:Xx) where "X" is the column and "x" is the row.

The locations can span any number of data locations and everything in between will be included in the average value.

The operand for a range of locations is the colon ":". The range can be used in the vertical or the horizontal direction.

	MON	TUES	TOTAL SALES
FISH	6	4	10
BEEF	3	5	8
DAY TOTAL	6	9	18

What many people don't realize is that the SUMMATION formula can be used diagonally for areas of numbers.

In the spreadsheet example above, we have taken the average spanning the blocks from "MON" and "FISH" to the location "TUES" and "BEEF".

You can see that the total sales were 18 units. Your unit sales are simply the sum of "6+3+4+5".

So we have used the SUMMING operand across the diagonal span of values and captured more than one row and column in the equation. This can save you a lot of separate formulas where one would do.

Note: Before you mix different mathematical operations, unless you are adept at using Excel, do not rely on the order of operations that Excel follows when evaluating a formula. Always use parenthetical expressions to force the formula to do your calculations in the order you intend.

SUBTRACTION

To find the difference between two or more locations that are not adjacent to one another, use the formula;

=SUM(Xx-Xx)

Now you say, "Hey! Wait! That's addition, not subtraction." You're right. There is no such arithmetic function as subtraction in Excel.

Microsoft decided not to create a subtraction formula for Excel. Subtraction is an addition of positive and negative numbers.

In a way that's good, because now you can mix multiple addition and subtraction functions in a single formula, such as;
=SUM(B1-A2+C1)

Don't do that!

It's bad form. Excel interprets it as;

=SUM((B1-A2)+C1) which might be (10-5)+5, but you can't count on the formula being interpreted properly. Always use parenthetical expressions when subtracting with more than two numbers involved.

There is a major difference between the following two expressions.

=SUM((10-5)+5) which equals 10

and

=SUM(10-(5+5)) which equals zero.

So never do this =SUM(10-5+5)

While Microsoft insists that there is no subtract function, you can still enter the formula =(Xx-Xx) so in the absence of a function name, the "SUM" function is implied.

MULTIPLICATION

To multiply two or more locations whether or not they are adjacent to one another, use the formula;

=Xx*Xx where "X" is the letter at the head of the column and "x" is the row number.

The operand for a multiplication of any two locations is obviously the asterisk "*". The values can be used in the vertical or the horizontal direction.

You're beginning to realize that with all the parenthetical equations, you are going to have to brush up on your high school algebra.

The math shouldn't be as scary as you might think at first. You are probably just automating the same math you have been doing with a calculator, ledger or pad, and pencil. You are already applying the math every day, but from now on, let the computer do the grunt work. Use the free time to take your dog for a walk or brush up on your golf swing (why do people play golf anyway?).

Note: Before you mix different mathematical operations, be sure you use a parenthetical equation in the formula. Once again, make no assumptions about the order of execution. One error in the assumption can be disastrous.

DIVISION

Division is much like subtraction in that there is no declarative function. To find the dividend of two or more locations that are not adjacent to one another, use the formula;

(Xx/Xx) where "X" is the letter at the head of the column and "x" is the row number.

So, like subtraction or multiplication, there is no clearly defined qualifier.

The reason there is a SUM or AVERAGE qualifier is because we can simply span a column or an area of cells without using the plus sign between each cell as in =SUM(Xx:Xx), but you can't so easily do the same with the other functions.

With the divide function it is either isolated as a simple expression identified by the math symbol "/", or embedded in a parenthetical expression.

CHAPTER 6 CHARTS and GRAPHS?

While spreadsheets are excellent for displaying trends, balancing the books and otherwise creating a matrix of information, charts and graphs can more clearly convey other types of information.

Let's take a look at just a few of the more fundamental types. There are a few we won't be going over in this book. That's because this is much like a college 101 course to familiarize you with Excel, not a high level or in depth study.

THE BAR CHART

Bar charts are one of the most common ways to display data. They have the advantage of giving you visual comparisons at a glance, such as total sales.

Each of the bars shares a common identity and is of relative amplitude to a common metric.

Bar charts can also be used in place of pie charts when the elements are too numerous for a pie.

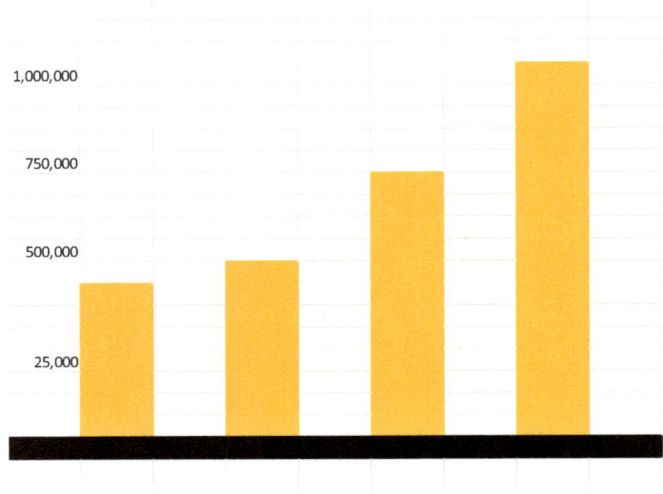

The chart above represents total sales.

THE STACKED BAR CHART
The stacked bar chart is used when presenting volume within one area as compared to other areas also having internal comparisons. They have the advantage of giving you visual comparisons at a glance.

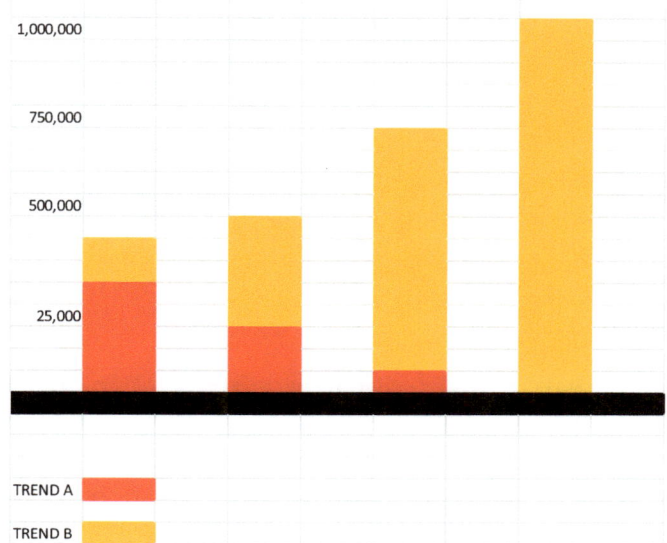

The chart above shows the downward sales trend for TREND A while showing the increasing sales trend for TREND B, while also showing the upward trend in total sales. It allows for the presentation of more than one element in a single chart.

THE LINE CHART

Line charts are also one of the most frequently used chart types. Line charts connect individual numeric data points.

Rather than compare similar characteristics by comparing the amplitude of the data, they plot trends. A line chart can compare trends by having unique plot lines for each item being compared.

Line charts have the advantage of not only comparing amplitude, but can compare amplitude across a given trend line, such as time.

THE PIE CHART

Pie charts show the viewer relative percentages or proportions at a glance.

They are color coded or texture coded to highlight the different elements of the "pie".

Although pie charts are the most frequently misused of all the chart styles, they are mostly beneficial when you have a half dozen or less elements, and the few comparative proportions are less ambiguous than a bar chart.

The pie chart answers the question, "What part of the whole does each piece comprise?"

By now you're wondering how to make your own charts. It's easier than you might think. The hard part of making charts is the organization of your spreadsheet so that when you create the chart, it will make some sense.

MAKING YOUR OWN CHARTS

Let's make a simple spreadsheet and create a chart.

I have chosen book sales as an example of something we might want to plot. The chart below shows the number of each type of book being sold in our fictitious book store.

We have broken books down into three types, eBooks, paperbacks, and hard cover.

Then we break sales down into three categories, morning, noon and evening sales. This will give us some feeling for how many people will buy books on the way to work, at lunchtime or after work.

	Morning	Noon	Evening
EBooks	22	32	65
Sft Cvr	23	22	95
Hrd Cvr	12	32	32

To create a chart, you just put the mouse pointer in the upper left corner of the area you want to chart, then while holding the left mouse button down, drag the pointer to the lower right hand corner of the area you want to chart and release the button.

The area you want to chart is darkened.

Now go to the top of the Excel spreadsheet and select the "INSERT" function. Then click on the "CHARTS" group so we can show all the various types of charts available.

Now select a chart type. I have selected the "COLUMN" chart.

When you select the "COLUMN" chart, a box drops down showing all the types of column charts available. I have chosen the first (simplest) type.

The resulting chart is shown below.

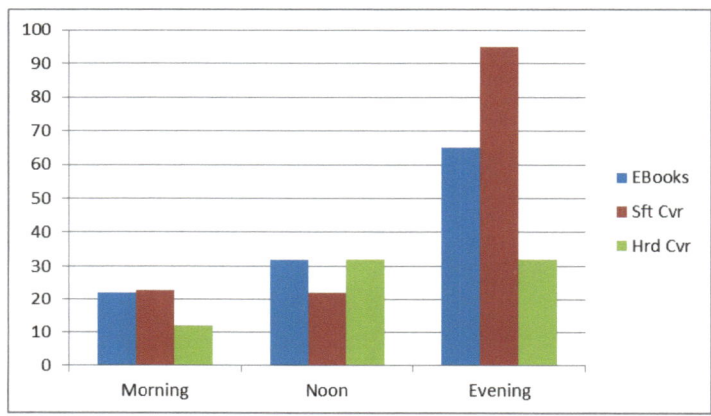

The resulting column chart is shown above. The Excel program will assign colors to the various types of books and plot them according to the time of day.

The vertical gradient on the left edge of the chart represents number of books.

You can now see at a glance the time of day when book sales are most prevalent and the types of books sold during those times.

Another type of chart we could choose is the pie chart, but you can also see that might be a mistake based on the lack of clarity around the exact number of books sold and the time of day the sales occurred.

How do we switch from the column chart to the pie chart? You can try every type of chart until you settle on the type of chart you like.

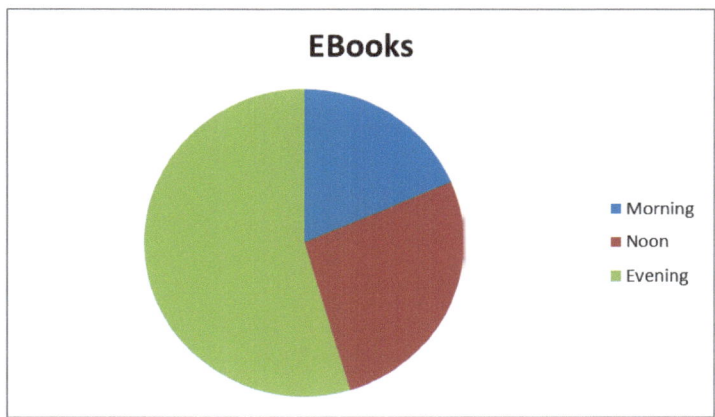

Just put your mouse pointer on the chart you have created and right click on it. A drop down menu appears and on the list of options, it says, "Change chart type...". Click on this and all of the chart types are made available for you to select.

When you have selected the desired chart type, it will appear.

While this chapter is called "Charts **and** Graphs" the next chapter is called "Charts **or** Graphs". In the next chapter we will talk about which chart to use and when.

So let's try another type. We right click on the pie chart and select a line graph.

The resulting line graph is shown below and once again we can see that it isn't as clear as the column chart we created in the beginning.

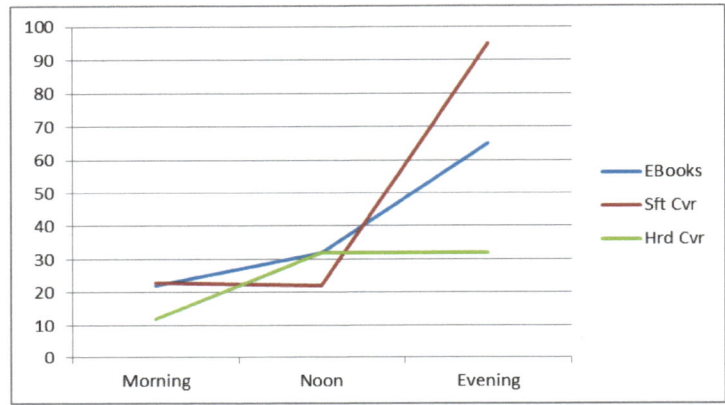

There is just too much work for our eyes to do here for us to properly quantify the data.

So let's take a look at the rationale behind the type of charts to be used and under what circumstances.

CHAPTER 7 CHARTS or GRAPHS

When to use bar charts:

Comparing data in a single data type, usually across time, but may include other factors.

The stacked bar chart is used to do a double comparison, such as sales by type of item vs. total sales.

When to use line charts:

Plotting trends, usually over time, but can be used in other application, such as freezing point temperature over a range of a given compound concentration, such as antifreeze..

When to use pie charts:

Showing comparative proportions where the total equals 100%. Pie charts can be used for anything from money to acreage.

It is generally agreed that if you have more than six proportions to communicate, consider a bar chart.

Other types of charts:

This introductory tutorial addresses the basics of Excel and is not intended to branch out into all of the chart types, but I have given you some idea of the charts you can make using Excel.

Other types of charts are, the MAP. SCATTER/PLOT, GANTT, and the BUBBLE chart. There are many more than these listed here.

CHAPTER 8 PRINTER LAYOUT

It can be aggravating when you print your spreadsheet and it spans more than one page across and more than one page tall.

There are ways to force the spreadsheet to fit the page. This chapter is dedicated to making your printed report look good.

The first obvious remedy is to change the print layout from portrait to landscape. That's done after clicking on "File", then "Print" and selecting "Orientation", then choosing "Landscape".

Regrettably there is no way to force a spreadsheet to fit the page if it is oversized.

The spreadsheet will insert dotted lines to indicate the edge of the print areas when building the data areas. Plan ahead. After all, the printed outcome is the product you are creating.

CHAPTER 9 APPLY SPREADSHEETS

Excel does magic when it comes to keeping track of numbers, but that's only a small part of what Excel can do for you.

The matrix of cells can be used to create a perfect layout of information in grid form so you can see the status of a number of items at once.

	USB DRIVE	FLOPPY DISK	CD ROM	DVD ROM
Song of the Flowers	YES	YES		YES
September Song		YES	YES	YES
Winter's Refrain	YES	YES		YES
Falling Leaves	YES		YES	

It's obvious at a glance which songs are recorded on which type of media in the spreadsheet above.

If your intent is to record every one of the four songs on each and every one of the four types of media, a spreadsheet would map the project most easily.

This simple example of a non-numeric plot illustrates the value of this approach. There are far more complex situations in the business environment crying out for the simple method shown here. Restaurant food inventory is another perfect example of the use of a non-numeric spreadsheet that could be modified to flag shortages in any of the major food types.

breads	rolls	86	14 italian	22	-2 french	12	4 sandwitch	33	27
veggies	lettice	12	18 peas	22	0 corn	22	6 medley	33	3
starches	potato	66	0 rice	23	12 pasta	34	10 lasagnia	23	2
pasteries	pie	34	-4 cake	22	3 donuts	34	10 cookies	54	12

The spreadsheet shown above is an example of a hybrid chart, where there is a blend of arithmetic and non-arithmetic functions.

The inventory level requirement is not directly shown, but is included in the formula for the cell for each discrete product.

The formula for each cell is "=SUM(n-Xx) where n=number of units required and Xx is the number of units on hand, and the number in red is the difference.

So there is an overstock of pies and Italian bread (negative values). No units need to be ordered for potato or corn (both at zero).

All the rest of the product needs to be ordered in the volumes shown in red to replenish the stock.

If the number of units required changes, you need only modify the formula.

If the number of units on hand changes at the end of the day, you change the number shown in black to indicate the units on hand.

This simple sheet will make your inventory maintenance a breeze and will reduce both the effort to restock the kitchen and reduce errors, because the numbers are so clearly listed in the report.

Having the right tools on hand to monitor and control a process will enable you to dramatically reduce errors.

CHAPTER 10 SPREADSHEET HISTORY

VisiCalc for the Apple II was the first computer spreadsheet program to hit the market in 1979. It was then ported over to the IBM PC/XT in 1981.

VisiCalc was the first software to combine all the features of a modern spreadsheet program, having a WYSIWYG (What You See Is What You Get) interactive user interface. VisiCalc was the first program to make the IBM PC a valued business system.

VisiCalc was responsible for the success of both the IBM PC and the Apple II. Lotus 1-2-3 followed suit and then other DOS applications.

The acceptance of the IBM PC was slow to be accepted because people thought the computer was a fad. Most of the programs available for it were ported over from other larger computer platforms.

Then Lotus 1-2-3 came along in 1983 written for the IBM PC. Lotus 1-2-3 outperformed the Apple II with VisiCalc and captured the market along with the IBM PC..

Microsoft entered the market with Excel in early 1990. Excel outperformed Lotus 1-2-3.

Microsoft created the Office Suite in the 1990s.

Now we have Gnumeric and Open Office Suite which are both free open source applications

ABOUT THE AUTHOR

I am a retired hardware and software Engineer with a background in Law Enforcement and real estate brokerage.

Log onto my Web Site for a link to other books I have written;

http://WWW.RobStetson.Com

www.ingramcontent.com/pod-product-compliance
Lightning Source LLC
Chambersburg PA
CBHW041112180526
45172CB00001B/224